WELCOME TO ZOO 3D

by

David E. Klutho

FOREWORD
PAGE 6

MAMMALS
PAGE 8

BIRDS
PAGE 42

INSECTS
PAGE 52

AMPHIBIANS
PAGE 58

WHO'S WHO AT THE ZOO
PAGE 70

REPTILES
PAGE 62

JUST FOR FUN!
PAGE 75

way Foreword ron magill zoo miami

Two of my greatest passions in life are animals and photography. As a young boy, nature images, combined with many trips to the zoo, inspired me to seek a career with wildlife that I have been privileged to have for more than 30 years. Having an up-close experience such as this one with Fezzik (and his extraordinary tongue) is one of the many wonderful opportunities I have enjoyed.

Thanks to the incredible skill and vision of David Klutho, readers can now take a trip to the zoo and have the animals jump off the page! His state-of-the-art 3D photography invites you to reach through each "window" he has created to touch the subjects while feeling like you are part of the shot!

This is a magical trip to the zoo like you've never experienced before!

BINOCULAR VISION

Predator

Prey

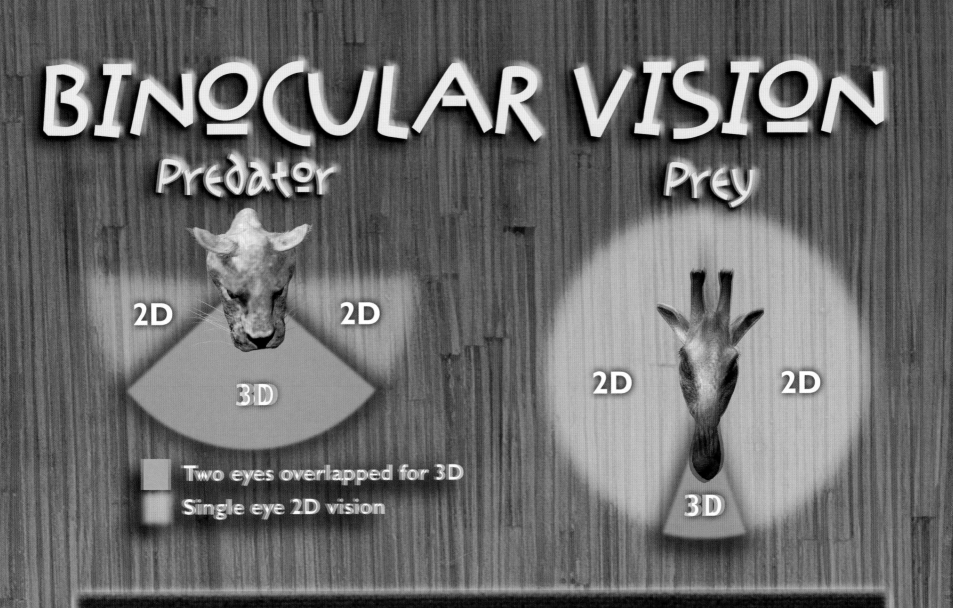

2D 2D

3D

2D 2D

3D

Two eyes overlapped for 3D
Single eye 2D vision

HOW DO animals see? Some animals (including humans) have stereoscopic (3D), or binocular, vision. Creatures with this type of sight have both eyes at the front of the head, facing forward, so the visual fields, or the areas they see in front of them, overlap. The brain processes the overlapped images three-dimensionally, which helps these animals with their depth perception, enabling them to judge distances accurately. The field of vision of animals who have stereoscopic sight is narrow (about 180°) compared with animals with monocular (2D) vision.

Predators such as lions, owls, and dogs usually have stereoscopic vision.

Animals with monocular vision have eyes on both sides of the head. The visual fields of creatures with monocular vision have little or no overlapping. Animals with monocular vision can see images two-dimensionally, which helps them detect enemies from all around (even from behind). The field of vision of animals with monocular vision is wide (almost 360°). Prey such as giraffes, rabbits, and pigeons usually have monocular vision.

ron labbe
studio 3D

MAMMALS

Mammals can be as tiny as a bee-size bat or as humongous as a whale. There are mammals that fly and mammals that swim in the seas. Mammals live in every habitat and on every continent. As diverse as they are, mammals have a few things in common. They are warm-blooded and have hair. Mammals raise their young until the young can survive on their own. Mammal moms feed milk to their offspring. And mammals have large brains, so they are pretty smart, as can be seen in dolphins, chimpanzees—and humans!

Grizzly Bear

BEAR NECESSITIES Grizzly bears got their name from the word *grizzled,* which means having hair streaked with gray. The fur of some grizzly bears is light-colored. But many grizzlies have brown fur, and in fact the grizzly is a type of brown bear. Grizzlies are found in the northwestern U.S., Alaska, and western Canada, as well as in northern parts of Europe and Asia. They are a threatened species in the Lower 48. Grizzlies live along coasts, and in mountainous and grassy areas. Weighing as much as 1,700 pounds, and measuring five to eight feet long, these bears are big. Their long claws are used mostly to dig up plants to eat. They also chow down on small animals, and many grizzlies love fish, especially salmon.

Grizzly Bear Cubs

SCOUTING CUBS During winter, grizzly moms give birth in dens while they are hibernating, or sleeping. Grizzly cubs are usually born in pairs, and with no teeth, almost no fur, and eyes that don't open for more than a month. Baby bears don't cry. Instead, they hum—loudly enough to be heard outside the den. The cute cubs stay by their mother's side for more than two years before heading out on their own.

DID YOU KNOW?

An image of a grizzly bear appears on the California state flag. Unfortunately, grizzlies are extinct in that state. The last one there was killed in 1922.

Asiatic Black Bear

SEE SPOT CLIMB There are more black bears than any other type of bear in the world. But only the Asiatic black bear has a V-shaped white spot on its chest. Found in many areas of Asia, it lives in mountain forests, where it climbs trees to feast on nuts, fruits, and flowers. Sometimes, it builds nests in the branches for dozing.

Koala

Koalas aren't bears. They are marsupials—animals such as kangaroos and opossums that carry their babies in pouches.

Polar Bear

FUR REAL The largest meat-eaters on land, polar bears live in the frozen Arctic. A thick layer of fat and heavy waterproof fur keep them warm—even when swimming for miles searching for prey in frigid waters.

DID YOU KNOW?

The polar bear's fur looks white, but it is actually transparent. The hairs are hollow, and when the sun's rays reflect off them, they appear white—just like ice and snow do.

Wolf's Guenon

MONKEY BUSINESS

Living in tropical forests in Africa, these active, sociable monkeys communicate with each other through different sounds and facial expressions. They eat fruit, insects, and small animals. When they find more food than they can eat, they store it in large pouches in their mouths.

Giant Panda

PANDA-MONIUM People love pandas, mostly because they're chubby, have black-and-white fur, and sit upright when eating. These endangered creatures live in forests in the mountains of central China, where their main food source grows—bamboo plants.

Orangutan

SWINGERS Unlike other apes, orangutans have orange hair, and they spend most of their time in trees instead of on the ground. Their long arms span more than seven feet, and their feet work like hands, letting them grip branches tightly. Orangutans live in the tropical rain forests of Borneo and Sumatra, two islands in Southeast Asia. These endangered apes are so smart, zookeepers have a hard time keeping them from escaping their enclosures.

Bonobo

AWESOME APE Found in one small area of central Africa, these apes look like slightly smaller chimps. But they don't always act like chimps: Bonobos have a more vegetarian diet, rarely fight among themselves, and walk more easily on two legs. Bonobos are intelligent: They can use twigs, sticks, and rocks as tools to scoop up termites or break open nuts. Bonobos share food and look out for each other when danger threatens. They may be the smartest of the apes, but they are also one of the most endangered. Few remain in the wild.

DID YOU KNOW?

Bonobos were named incorrectly after a place called Bolobo. The village is located in Africa, in the Democratic Republic of Congo. This is the only place bonobos exist in the wild. In Africa, a bonobo is called an *elia*.

DID YOU KNOW?

A langur has a large stomach that enables it to digest tough food. Special bacteria in the stomach also help it break down leaves, flowers, and fruit. A gland that produces lots of saliva helps too.

Ebony Langur

MONKEY BUSINESS

Langur means "long tail" in Hindi, an official language of India. That name fits these monkeys perfectly: Their tales are nearly twice as long as their bodies. Ebony langurs live mostly in the rain forests of Java, an island of Indonesia. Known as leaf monkeys, they stay high up in trees during the day, eating their favorite food—you guessed it—leaves!

Hamadryas Baboon

FUNKY MONKEY Baboons are large monkeys that live mostly on the ground. Hamadryas baboons are found in dry, rocky areas in East Africa and the Middle East. They live in families that join together to form troops, which can consist of hundreds of hamadryas. A male leads and controls groups of baboons with the threat of his large, sharp front teeth.

Western Lowland Gorilla

GENTLE GIANT The western lowland gorilla is the smallest of several species of gorilla. But it's no shrimp, standing five and a half feet tall and weighing up to 400 pounds. Gorillas are powerful, but these mainly plant-eaters are shy, smart, and mostly peaceful. Western lowland gorillas live in tropical forests in Africa in groups called troops. A troop is led by the biggest male, known as a silverback, named for the silver hair that grows on its back and sides.

DID YOU KNOW?

When a gorilla seems to yawn, it's nervous, not tired. If it still feels threatened, it barks, throws plants, and beats its chest. If that doesn't work, the gorilla will charge and knock over or bite the threat.

Greater One-Horned Rhinoceros

HORNING IN This rhinoceros lives in the forests, grasslands, and wetlands of India and Nepal. It is 12 feet long, weighs more than 4,000 pounds, and sports a single horn that can grow as long as two feet. The rhino looks like an armored tank because its skin hangs in heavy folds that resemble metal plates. And small lumps on the skin look like rivets. The rhino eats lots of grass, as well as fruit and leaves. It also likes to wallow in water to cool off. This rhino species was once almost extinct because of hunters and the destruction of the animal's habitat. But thanks to conservation programs, about 2,000 rhinos of this species still live in the wild.

DID YOU KNOW?

The greater one-horned rhino is also called an Indian rhino. It is one of three types of Asian rhinoceros. The other two, the Sumatran and Javan, are found in Southeast Asia and are critically endangered.

White Rhinoceros

CRASH COURSE

A group of rhinoceroses is called a crash. That's because these huge beasts crash their way through the grasslands of Africa. The white rhino is the biggest of all rhino species. Thirteen feet long, six feet tall, and sometimes weighing 6,000 pounds, it can be as heavy as three cars. A white rhino can move at nearly 25 miles per hour. Its giant head can weigh as much as 1,000 pounds. The white rhino has two horns. The front horn can reach six feet in length. This horn is valuable for defense, but unfortunately, it is also valuable to some humans. Poachers kill rhinos for their horns, which are used—mistakenly—as medicine.

South American Coati

RINGED LEADER Coatis like this one are members of the raccoon family—small furry animals with a ring pattern on their tails. This species lives both in trees and on the ground, and is found in forests in Central and South America. The coati pokes its long nose into any place there might be food—which, for a coati, can be anything from berries to mice.

Meerkat

MOB RULE Meerkats believe in togetherness. These small, catlike animals work in groups to survive on the plains of southern Africa. They live in large families called mobs, in underground burrows. Meerkat moms share in raising babies, even those not their own. Meerkats attack large prey, like lizards, as a group. When a mob goes out to hunt, adults take turns acting as lookouts. They give a warning call when trouble nears, so the mob can run back to the burrow.

Nile Hippopotamus

POSITIVELY **NO** SWIMMING

HIPPO, HIPPO, HOORAY! At up to 8,000 pounds, the hippopotamus is one of the heaviest land animals on Earth. A hippo is happiest cooling off in the lakes and rivers of Africa. With ears and eyes on the top of its snout, this vegetarian can see and hear while mostly submerged. On land, a hippo produces a thick, pink fluid that covers it skin. The gunk acts like sunscreen and also kills germs.

California Sea Lion

LION AROUND These smart, hefty marine mammals spend most of their time along Pacific Ocean coastlines. They come ashore in large groups during mating season, barking loudly. These 1,000-pounders lumber on land but move smoothly in the sea. They swim at speeds up to 25 miles per hour and can stay underwater for 10 minutes. A layer of fat called blubber keeps them toasty in cold waters and provides energy.

DID YOU KNOW?

Sea lions are smart and can be taught to do entertaining behaviors by humans. That's why they perform in many marine parks and zoos.

Asian Small-Clawed Otter

OTTER-LY AMAZING A strong tail propels this sleek otter through freshwater streams and along coastal areas in Asia. The world's smallest species of otter, it has small claws, and its front paws are not completely webbed. That lets the handlike paws grasp objects better. The otter uses its paws to locate shellfish, such as crabs, hidden under rocks and mud. The otter's powerful teeth can crush shells to get at the food inside.

Maned Wolf

A LEG UP This wolf gets its name from the mane of fur along its back. Found in South America, the maned wolf lives by itself rather than in packs. Its habitat is mostly grasslands, to which its long legs are well suited. Standing tall, the wolf can peer over tall grass to spot prey. This shy night hunter is endangered.

Cougar

NAME GAME Also called a puma, panther, and mountain lion, this big cat roams from Canada to southernmost South America. Its has the largest range of any land mammal in the Western Hemisphere.

Cheetah

SPEED THRILLS The cheetah is the world's fastest land animal. It can sprint as fast as 68 miles per hour. After a minute of running, the cheetah has to rest and cool its 125-pound body. The big cat hangs out in grasslands in Africa, south of the Sahara. Here, the open spaces make it easier for it to chase down gazelles, warthogs, and other small animals.

African Lion

GIRL POWER The lion may be the king of the jungle, but his maneless mate keeps the kingdom running. Female lions, their offspring, and a few males live together in a group called a pride. The females do most of the hunting for a pride. They work together to bring down wildebeest, zebras, and other large animals. Female lions also raise the cubs without help from the males. Male lions do defend the pride—and at 550 pounds and 10 feet in length, they are more than a match for anything but other lions. The big cats roam the plains and woodlands of Africa (and one small area of India). Most live in protected parks and game preserves. Otherwise, these incredible cats might one day disappear.

DID YOU KNOW?

The snow leopard sometimes wraps itself in its bushy tail, which is as long as its body. It uses the tail like a thick wool scarf to keep warm.

Snow Leopard

THE HIGH LIFE This endangered cat lives in central Asia, in remote mountains as high as 18,000 feet. A snow leopard is hard to spot—its black and gray fur blends in with the snowy background. The creature has no trouble scrambling along cold cliffs: A thick coat of fur keeps it warm; big furry paws act like snowshoes; and a long tail helps keep it balanced. The snow leopard can leap as far as 50 feet to grab prey, such as mountain goats and sheep.

Sumatran Tiger

ON THE PROWL The Sumatran tiger is found only on Sumatra, an island of Indonesia. The cat's color is darker than that of other tigers. That allows it to blend into the forests it prowls. Extra-long whiskers help it feel its way through thick underbrush.

DID YOU KNOW?

The Sumatran tiger is critically endangered. Fewer than 500 are left in the wild. Destruction of habitat and poaching, or illegal killing, are the main reasons so few exist.

White Tiger

SO WHITE A white tiger is a Bengal tiger with white fur. A change in a gene, called a mutation, causes the white coloring. White tigers are rare in the wild, but many have been bred in captivity.

Clouded Leopard

CLOUDY FUTURE? Native to the tropical rain forests of Southeast Asia, clouded leopards weigh only about 40 pounds and are three feet long. But their front teeth are two inches long—about the same size as a tiger's. Clouded leopards also have big feet and claws, which they use to climb trees. Walking headfirst down trees or hanging upside down by their back legs is a snap for these cats. The clouded leopard is rare in the wild—and even in zoos.

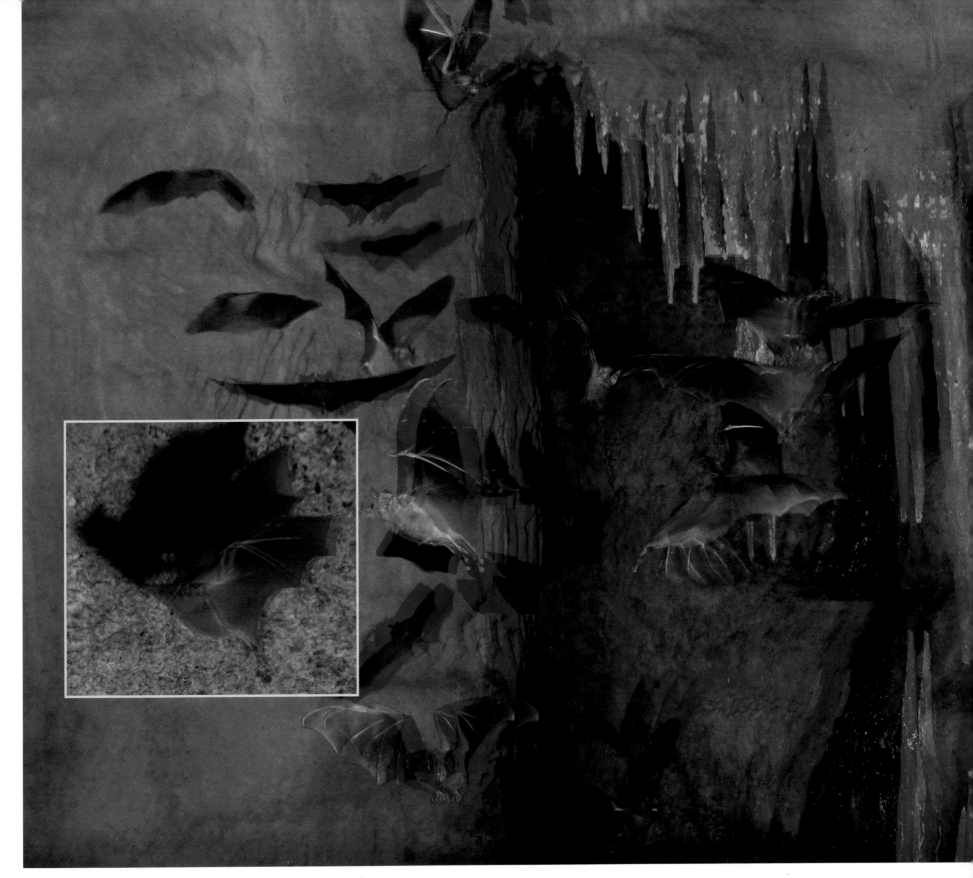

Fruit Bats

GOING BATTY Fruit bats find food mostly through sharp senses of smell and sight. At night, the short-tailed and Jamaican fruit bats shown here fly out in search of figs and other sweet fruit in the tropical forests of Central and South America. They help regrow forests by spitting out thousands of seeds daily or by leaving them in droppings.

Giant Anteater

TONGUE-TIED This Central and South American mammal has a long snout—and an even longer tongue. It sticks the two-foot-long tongue into a termite nest to slurp up a meal.

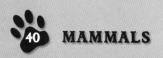

African Elephant

TRUNK SPACE Ten feet tall and weighing 13,000 pounds, the African elephant is the world's largest land animal. Found on the grasslands and in the forests of Africa, it is smart and sensitive. And yes, elephants have a good memory: They can recognize other elephants after being apart for many years.

Birds

Guira Cuckoo

NEST EGG The guira cuckoo likes to put all its eggs in one basket, er, nest. Groups of these spiky-haired South American birds lay as many as 20 eggs in a single nest. The birds also hang out together in bunches at night to stay warm.

Birds are warm-blooded animals that lay eggs. But what makes them special is their ability to wing it. A bird has hollow bones, thin legs, and a beak instead of a heavy jaw and teeth. Those features make a bird light enough for flight. And, of course, a bird has feathers and wings. Strong chest muscles make the wings flap, which enable a bird to take off. Feathers help give birds lift and make their bodies smooth, so they can cut through the air. The feathers also keep birds warm. Because birds can fly long distances to find food, they live just about everywhere on Earth. Of the 9,000 bird species, only a handful, such as the ostrich, kiwi and penguin, can't fly. The rest delight in flight.

DID YOU KNOW?

When moviemakers set a film in a jungle, they sometimes use the call of kookaburras on the soundtrack. That's because the cackling birds sound like monkeys.

Laughing Kookaburra

YOU'RE JOKING!

The kookaburra would be the perfect audience for a comedian. Native to Australia, the bird is famous for a call that sounds like a loud, slightly crazy human laugh. But the kookaburra's victims don't find the bird funny. The kookaburra waits on a branch for a snake or other animal to pass by on the ground. Then it flies down and snatches the prey in its strong beak. The bird swings the animal against a tree to kill it and make it easier to swallow.

Painted Stork

BILL, PLEASE! This three-foot-tall stork is found in tropical areas of Asia. It lives in large colonies near shallow bodies of freshwater, such as ponds and rivers. The painted stork has long legs, which it uses to wade into the water to find fish. The stork opens its big bill and swings it from side to side in the water. If the bill bumps into a fish, the bird snaps up the meal. Sometimes, the stork will use a wing to sweep fish into its bill.

DID YOU KNOW?

To take off into the air, pelicans must build up speed by running along the surface of the water.

Pink-Backed Pelican

BIG MOUTH Native to Africa and Asia, the pink-backed pelican is a great swimmer, thanks to its webbed toes. It is also an expert fisher. Its "net" is a large pouch of skin attached to the bottom of its long beak. The pelican swims on the water. When it sees fish below, it scoops up the catch of the day, along with about a gallon of water. The bird lets the water pour out of the pouch, then gulps down the meal.

Abyssinian Ground Hornbill

GROUNDED This African bird can fly, but it prefers to walk on the ground, searching for food. If threatened, the hornbill will walk or run away. It flies only when it's frightened or to avoid something in its path.

Ostrich

BIG BIRD Ostriches are the biggest, heaviest birds in the world. Males can be taller than seven feet and can weigh more than 300 pounds. Ostriches can't fly, but they can run—and fast. They can sprint up to 43 miles per hour to escape enemies on the plains and in the grasslands of Africa.

?

DID YOU KNOW?

An ostrich lays the biggest eggs of any bird. They can be six inches long and weigh about three pounds.

Eurasian Eagle Owl

WHAT A HOOT One of the largest owls in the world, the Eurasian eagle owl is more than two feet long. Found in Europe, North Africa, and Asia, this owl lives in various habitats, from forests to grasslands to dry areas. The Eurasian eagle owl is a night hunter. It flies quietly and uses its sharp sight and hearing to spot prey. Then it swoops down and grabs animals, including birds, in its long talons.

White-Breasted Cormorant

DIVE BOMBER The white-breasted cormorant is a seabird found in Africa, south of the Sahara desert. It lives either by the coasts or inland, near bodies of water containing fish. Zooming above the water, the bird dives for food. Strong webbed feet and a broad tail help it plunge more than 20 feet beneath the surface. The cormorant can stay underwater for about 40 seconds. After gulping down a large fish whole, the bird will stretch out to dry its feathers—and happily digest its meal.

Hyacinth Macaw

TRUE BLUE The biggest parrots are called macaws, and the biggest macaw is the hyacinth macaw. Found in South American forests, the bird has a five-foot wingspan and measures three feet from its bill to the tip of its tail. Its beak is strong enough to crush palm nuts, the macaw's favorite food. The bird's beautiful blue feathers are its most eye-catching feature.

DID YOU KNOW?

Only about 6,500 hyacinth macaws are left in the wild. That's because the birds are sold illegally as pets. A single bird can sell for as much as $12,000.

Humboldt Penguin

WADDLE YOU KNOW? A flightless bird, the Humboldt penguin has a streamlined body and wings that let it fly underwater at speeds reaching 30 miles per hour. These penguins live off the west coast of South America, where they gather in colonies near rocky shores. Humboldt penguins nest among boulders, in caves or burrows. Sometimes, they make a comfy but smelly home in a pile of guano, or bird droppings!

DID YOU KNOW?

Humboldt penguins aren't completely covered in feathers. They have pink patches around their faces and feet, and beneath their wings. The penguins live in a warm climate, and these bare patches of skin let them cool down.

Greater Flamingo

PRETTY IN PINK A flamingo uses its long legs to wade and feed in shallow lakes and lagoons. In cold water, it often stands on one leg so heat doesn't leave its body through its feet.

iNSECTS AND ARACHNIDS

Brazilian Giant Cockroach

COLOSSAL COCKROACH

There are more than 4,000 species of cockroach, and this is one of the biggest. Four inches long, it is found in tropical areas of Central and South America. The roach eats any kind of organic matter. And it avoids being eaten by giving off a nasty smell. If that doesn't work, it scuttles away.

There are anywhere from 2 million to 20 million different insect species—more than all other animal species combined. Insects are usually small, but some are larger than you might expect—or than you'd ever want to run into. For example, the titan beetle is more than six inches long! Many insects can fly, and most live on land, though some live in freshwater. Insects have six legs, three main body parts, and no skeleton. They are protected by a hard outer covering. Some insects are loners, but others, such as bees and ants, live in vast colonies. Wherever we live, except in the coldest places on Earth, insects are sure to be our neighbors.

Arachnids have eight legs and two body parts. Spiders are arachnids, and so are scorpions, ticks, and mites. There are about 70,000 species of arachnid, and most eat prey or are parasites that suck a prey's blood.

Gray Bird Grasshopper

HOP TO IT With the ability to jump 20 times its own length and wings that can carry it great distances, this grasshopper gets around. A plant-eater, it lives in the southern areas of North America. When gray bird grasshoppers fly in a swarm, they will chow down on most any vegetation in their path. How do they keep from being eaten? On the ground, their dark color blends into the brown earth.

Chilean Rose Tarantula

HAIRY SITUATION

A tarantula is a large, hairy spider. This jumbo species is found mostly in deserts in Chile, Bolivia, and Argentina, countries in South America. It lives in an underground burrow and comes out at night to kill prey with its poisonous fangs. When threatened, it kicks its hairs at an enemy, causing irritation and pain. The hairs also detect air movement and determine temperature. You might think this crawler is creepy, but it's a popular pet. Go figure!

Clipper Butterfly

SPOT ON This fast-flying butterfly lives in tropical forests in Southeast Asia. It got its name because the white spots on its wings look like the sails of an old-time clipper ship.

Hissing Cockroach

BOO, HISS! Snakes can hiss and people can, too. But a cockroach? This cockroach produces different hissing sounds, indicating anger, alarm, or that it's in the mood to mate. The sound is so loud, it can be heard 12 feet away! This cockroach is unusual in a few other ways. It is found only on the island of Madagascar, in the Indian Ocean. It is a really hardy roach—growing up to three inches long. And get this: The male has horns on its head that it uses to butt other cockroaches during battle!

African Moon Moth

FULL MOON Most moths are dull-looking. But the African moon moth has style. It is green, has markings like eyes on its wings, comes with two tails, and is very large. Its wingspan is about four and a half inches, and it is about five and a half inches from head to "tails." Hanging from a branch, it looks like a leaf. If a predator gets close, the moth's "eyes" might freak it out.

Crickets

JIMINY! Crickets love to sing! They produce a loud, chirping song by rubbing one wing against the other. Males chirp at night to attract females, and the noise can be heard as far away as a mile. Crickets are found almost everywhere in the world. In warm weather, they live in fields and woods. When it gets cold, they sometimes climb into houses and serenade people who are trying to sleep.

DID YOU KNOW?

When an African moon moth becomes an adult, it doesn't eat. It doesn't even have a mouth, so it lives for only about a week—just long enough to mate.

AMPHIBIANS

File-Eared Tree Frog

RIBBITING! This frog lives in rain forests in Indonesia and Malaysia—countries in Southeast Asia. It spends days perched on a branch above a pool of water. Sticky foot pads and long, thin legs let it move easily from one branch to another. The female even lays eggs in the branches, in a nest made of foam.

Amphibians lead double lives. These animals can live both in the water and on land. Some amphibians start out as tiny tadpoles that swim in the water and breathe through gills. As the tadpoles grow, they develop features—such as lungs—that let them hang out on land. But many amphibians also take in oxygen through their thin, smooth skin, so they need to stay moist. Also, these critters usually lay eggs in water. So amphibians must live in damp places, near rivers or ponds—or even in the wet air of a rain forest. These cold-blooded creatures don't produce their own heat. That's one reason frogs, toads, salamanders, and other amphibians often live in warm areas.

DID YOU KNOW?

This tiger's stripes let it blend into the surroundings. For more protection, the salamander has glands that give off poison, making it a deadly meal.

Tiger Salamander

STRIPE A POSE Growing up to 14 inches in length, this tiger is large—for a salamander. It is found in forests and dry brushlands throughout North America. Tiger salamanders live in underground burrows, and when it rains, they make their way to ponds and other small bodies of water to breed.

Albino American Bullfrog

Amazon Milk Tree Frog

GOT POISON? High in the trees in the rain forests of South America, the Amazon milk frog sleeps during the day and hunts for insects at night. Large disks at the ends of its fingers enable the frog to grip branches or stems—even when it's asleep. It uses a long snout to push its way into a pile of leaves or branches to hide from enemies. If that doesn't work, a fearful frog has one more trick: Its skin can give off a milky-looking poison that is one big yech! to predators.

Golden Frog

SIGN LANGUAGE This frog's yellow or orange skin is a warning to enemies: Keep away! The skin produces a poison when the frog's in danger. If an animal bites into the frog, the pain will be a reminder never to try to eat it again. Golden frogs, which are endangered, live in the rain forests of Central America.

REPTILES

The giant dinosaurs that once ruled the Earth were reptiles. Plenty of reptiles are still around, but they're a lot smaller and a lot less scary. Like amphibians, reptiles are cold-blooded, sometimes live in water, and produce eggs. Unlike amphibians, reptiles usually lay their eggs on land, not in water. Reptiles live in deserts and other dry climates, but they are also found in wet and even cool regions. They can survive the heat because scales and tough skin hold in the body's water, helping to keep them cool. There are more than 8,000 species of reptile. Some, like turtles, have shells, and others have long tails and four legs. Still others, like snakes, have no limbs at all. The smallest reptile, a tiny chameleon, would fit on a fingertip. The largest, the saltwater crocodile, weighs 2,000 pounds!

Komodo Dragon

DRAGON'S TAIL The biggest and fiercest of all lizards is the Komodo dragon. It is found only on several small islands in the Asian nation of Indonesia. Komodos are about nine feet long, weigh 200 pounds, and can run 15 miles an hour. With razor-sharp teeth, they will devour large animals—and people, if they're not careful!

Grand Cayman Iguana

DID YOU KNOW?

The salifin lizard is a two-sport star. It not only swims fast, but it runs fast—along the surface of the water. Its secret? A sail-shaped fin down its back and tail helps it swim. And large, flat toes help it run on water.

Sailfin Lizard

ESCAPE ARTIST This lizard basks in the sun near watery areas in the Philippines, a nation in Southeast Asia. If a bird or other enemy comes close, the lizard makes a quick getaway. It drops off its branch or boulder into the water and swims away. If it isn't resting or swimming, the lizard is eating. It's omnivorous, which means it gobbles up both plants and animals.

Emerald Tree Boa

TIGHT SQUEEZE In the rain forests of South America, the six-foot-long emerald tree boa hangs by its tail from a branch, waiting. Suddenly, a bird or small mammal passes by. The boa darts out and grabs it in its teeth. Then the boa wraps its body around the victim. It squeezes hard until the animal dies. The boa swallows the animal whole. Yum!

Eyelash Viper

American Alligator

LATER GATOR This alligator is only two years old. Full-grown males are about 11 feet long and weigh up to 1,000 pounds. Alligators are similar to crocodiles: They both have scales, long jaws, and sharp teeth. How do you tell them apart? Gators have shorter, broader snouts than crocs. And when a gator's mouth is shut, the fourth lower tooth isn't visible. That tooth can be seen when a croc closes its mouth. Crocs are found mostly in Africa, Asia, and Australia (with a few types in Central and South America). Except for a species of alligator found in China, all gators live in North, Central, and South America.

Cuban Crocodile

CROC HOP This 10-foot-long croc lives in swamps on the Caribbean island of Cuba. Its powerful tail helps the crocodile leap out of the water to catch prey in low-hanging trees.

Radiated Tortoise

A FINE LINE The star of the tortoise world is the radiated tortoise. It has spectacular yellow lines that spread out, or radiate, from the center of each plate of its shell. To view this tortoise in the wild, go to Madagascar, an island in the Indian Ocean. But go soon—the tortoise is hunted for food and as a pet, and is very endangered.

Fly River Turtle

WATER HOG The Fly River turtle is also called the pig-nosed turtle—for good reason: Its snout looks like the snout of a pig. This turtle lives in the freshwaters of Australia and New Guinea. Swimming below the surface, it sticks its snout above the water to breathe. With paddle-like flippers instead of claws, and a smooth, streamlined shell, this turtle is made for marine life.

DID YOU KNOW?

Aborigines, the native people of Australia, drew pictures of Fly River turtles on rock walls 7,000 years ago.

WHO'S WHO AT THE ZOO

Meet some of the people who make a zoo work.

Star Attraction

Zoo visitors may get to see shows starring some of the zoo's creatures. The animals are taught behaviors by people who are both patient and expert at training wildlife. Here, Jennifer Lindsley of Zoo Miami shows off Sunny, a sulphur-crested cockatoo native to Australia. Sunny flies through hoops above the audience. The birds are prized pets in the U.S. but may wear out their welcome because of their destructive behavior and very loud screeching!

Meet the Public

One of the missions of a zoo is to educate the public about wildlife. Here, Jennifer Lindsley works with King George, a king cheetah. Captive-born in South Africa, King George was hand-raised by trainers at Zoo Miami so that he could be part of its Cheetah Ambassdor Program. The program takes cheetahs to places such as schools to teach people about these animals and encourage their protection. The king cheetah is distinguished by its large black blotches and the three or four stripes down its back instead of the small spots of a typical cheetah. There may be fewer than 50 king cheetahs in the world.

What's for Lunch?

Zookeeper Dolora Batchelor feeds American white pelicans at one of the lakes at Zoo Miami. The birds are fed lake smelt by hand so that Batchelor can make sure each one gets the proper amount of food. Creating this bond between the zookeeper and the birds also makes any future human handling easier.

For the Birds

Feeding time is important in all zoos, and zookeepers must make sure the animals are getting a balanced diet. In these photos, zookeeper Stephanie Casanova makes sure the nearly 400 birds in Zoo Miami's Wings of Asia aviary are getting just the right food. Their meals consist of a variety of items ranging from seeds and fruits to insects and fish. The meals are carefully prepared each day and distributed in specific areas within the aviary. Each morning, Casanova gives out the food while surveying the exhibit to account for each bird and then checking it off on a master list. This is an important process to help make sure that all the aviary's residents are doing well.

On the Mend

Chriss Miller, a zoo veterinarian, cleans a wound on a blue-billed curassow as she gets ready to re-bandage the bird's broken leg. The curassow sleeps peacefully thanks to anesthesia. The patient is also being carefully monitored by veterinary technician Rebeccah Mulder. The bird was found injured in its pen. It may have gotten its leg caught in some perches and broken it while trying to free itself. Thanks to the bird's excellent care, it is healing well. In the small photo, Dr. Miller studies the X-rays of the curassow's leg injury while holding the bird.

Just for FUN!
the D.A.V.I.D.

The 3D images on the next four pages are a little different from those in the rest of the book. They are made in a special way called **DIGITAL ANAGLYPHIC VERTICALLY INCLINED DISPLAY, OR D.A.V.I.D.** for short.

Here's how to view the following four pages in 3D: Lay the book flat on a table and put on your red-and-cyan 3D glasses. Then sit back so you can look at the image at a 45-degree angle, just as the boy on the right is doing. (If you looked straight down, that would be a 90-degree angle.) Now the picture will look like it's popping right out of the page!

Common
White-Eyed
Duck

Meerkat

Emperor
Scorpion

California
Sea Lion

THE ENDS